YELLOWSTONE NATIONAL PARK

A TRUE BOOK

by
David Petersen

Children's Press®
A Division of Scholastic Inc.

New York Toronto London Auckland Sydney
Mexico City New Delhi Hong Kong
Danbury, Connecticut

A waterfall at Yellowstone

Reading Consultant
Nanci R. Vargus, Ed.D.
Primary Multiage Teacher
Decatur Township Schools,
Indianapolis, IN

The photograph on the cover shows Mammoth Hot Springs at Yellowstone National Park. The photograph on the title page shows thermal hot springs at Yellowstone.

Library of Congress Cataloging-in-Publication Data

Petersen, David, 1946–
    Yellowstone National Park / by David Petersen.
        p. cm. — (A True book)
    Includes bibliographical references and index.
    ISBN 0-516-21668-6   0-516-27326-4 (pbk.)
    1. Yellowstone National Park—Juvenile literature. [1. Yellowstone
National Park. 2. National parks and reserves.] I. Title. II. Series.
F722 P48 2001
978.7'52—dc21

Contents

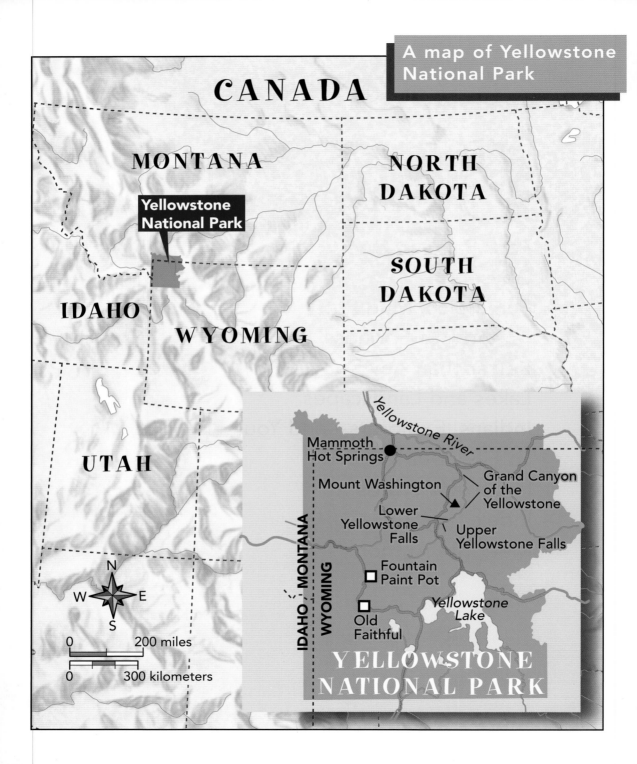

A map of Yellowstone National Park

CANADA

MONTANA

NORTH DAKOTA

Yellowstone National Park

SOUTH DAKOTA

IDAHO

WYOMING

UTAH

N
W E
S

0   200 miles

0   300 kilometers

Yellowstone River

Mammoth Hot Springs

Mount Washington

Grand Canyon of the Yellowstone

Lower Yellowstone Falls

Upper Yellowstone Falls

IDAHO | MONTANA

WYOMING

Fountain Paint Pot

Yellowstone Lake

Old Faithful

YELLOWSTONE NATIONAL PARK

Four Parks in One

There is no place on Earth like Yellowstone National Park. Yellowstone is in northwest Wyoming and spreads into Montana and Idaho. It is big, beautiful, wild, and wonderfully weird. In fact, Yellowstone is four parks in one: a thermal park, a wildlife park, a wilderness park, and a historical park.

Thermal means "caused by heat." At Yellowstone, the Earth's core of melted rock, called magma, lies closer to

Yellowstone has many unusual-looking natural formations.

Earth's surface than anywhere else in the world. Thousands of years ago, magma surged up through cracks to the surface and escaped in huge explosions, called volcanic eruptions.

When magma cools, it becomes lava rock. Lava rock is everywhere at Yellowstone. A volcano is a cone-shaped mountain of lava created by a

Lava rock at Yellowstone

Mount Washburn

volcanic eruption. Mount Washburn, the highest point in the park, is an ancient volcano.

Today, the same magma that caused Yellowstone's ancient volcanic eruptions heats the water that creates

One of Yellowstone's many hot springs

the park's thermal features. These include geysers, fumaroles, mud pots, and hot springs.

Geysers

Geysers are natural hot-water fountains. Yellowstone has nearly three hundred geysers, more than anywhere else on Earth.

When water from melted snow and rain trickles deep into the ground, it collects in pockets, or channels. There it

absorbs heat from the magma layer far below.

As the water warms, it expands, creating pressure. Some under-ground channels have a narrow spot—usually near the Earth's surface. This narrow spot causes the water below it to be under tremendous pressure. When the pressure is great enough, the water steams, boiling up through cracks to the surface.

Norris Geyser Basin at Yellowstone

Castle Geyser erupting

When all that hot water reaches the surface, it erupts into the air—like a water volcano. After enough pressure has been released, the geyser eruption ends, and the cycle begins again.

Yellowstone's most famous geyser is called Old Faithful. It erupts about every 78 minutes, creating a gushing fountain more than 100 feet (30.5 meters) high. Each eruption lasts about three minutes and could fill a swimming pool!

Old Faithful erupts about every 78 minutes.

Fumaroles, Mud Pots, and Hot Springs

In many parts of Yellowstone, steam and smelly gases spew out of the ground, like dozens of smoky campfires. These steamy vents are called *fumaroles*, from a Latin word meaning "smoke."

Sometimes, thermal steam rises through a mud puddle,

Fumaroles (above) and the Fountain Paint Pot (right) at Yellowstone

creating a bubbling, burping mud pot. When a mud pot is colored by minerals, it's called a paint pot.

Yellowstone's lakes and streams are cold, averaging 41° Fahrenheit (5° Celsius). A hot spring is created when steam rises through the cold water and warms it.

Often, colorful algae and bacteria live in hot springs, tinting the water orange, yellow, brown, or green.

Some hot springs, such as Grand Prismatic Pool, are colored by algae and bacteria.

Mammoth Hot Springs

Sometimes, hot springs carry minerals to the surface. Over time, these minerals harden and build up, making lovely terraces and steps. The largest of these at Yellowstone is Mammoth Hot Springs.

A Petrified Forest

In parts of Yellowstone Park, entire forests were buried by ancient volcanic eruptions. The ash and mud that covered the forests contained minerals. Slowly, the minerals were absorbed by the trees and turned to stone, creating petrified trees.

Erosion gradually wore away the soil surrounding the stone trees, exposing Yellowstone's famous petrified forests.

Better than Any Zoo

Yellowstone National Park is home today to almost every native wild animal that lived there when the first Europeans arrived.

The bison, or buffalo, is a giant, shaggy member of the cattle family. For centuries, bison provided everything

A bison herd at Yellowstone

needed by American Indians of the West—meat, clothing, and shelter. When white settlers arrived, they killed almost all the bison in America. Fortunately, a few were able to hide and survive at Yellowstone. Today, the park has one of the largest bison herds anywhere.

Like the bison, the prong-horn feeds in sagebrush flats. It is America's fastest runner. Although the pronghorn is often called an antelope, it is not. Antelope live only in Africa and Asia.

Yellowstone has more elk than any other place on Earth. Elk are giant members of the deer family. Every autumn, bull

Yellowstone is home to large numbers of pronghorn (above) and elk (left).

elk fill the park with loud, whistling bugle calls. Elk can also mew like cats and chirp like birds!

Moose like Yellowstone's marshy areas.

The largest deer of all, the moose, can be as big as a horse. Moose like marshy areas, where they browse on willow brush and aquatic plants.

Animals that eat other animals are called predators. People once thought predators were bad animals, and shot them on sight. By the mid-1920s, all of Yellowstone's gray wolves had been killed.

Today, we know that predators are necessary to the balance of nature. In the mid-1990s, wolves were returned to Yellowstone.

Gray wolves were brought back to Yellowstone in the 1990s.

After 70 years of unnatural silence, the park once again echoes with the joyful howling of wolves!

Despite their name, black bears may be brown, cinnamon, or even blond. Bears will eat almost anything—meat, grass, wildflowers, and human food. For their own safety as well as the bears', people should never leave food lying around in the open when camping in bear country. And Yellowstone is definitely bear country!

Grizzly bears are larger and fiercer than black bears. Yellowstone is one of only a few places left in the United

States where grizzlies still roam free. The grizzly gets its name from the silvery, or grizzled, color of its fur.

Yellowstone is home to many smaller animals too—including ground squirrels, prairie dogs, and chipmunks. Their predators include badgers, coyotes, foxes, and birds of prey such as hawks and owls.

Yellowstone is a bird-watching paradise, with blue-black ravens and snow-white pelicans,

(Clockwise from top left) Ground squirrels, prairie dogs, coyotes, and badgers are among the animals that can be found at Yellowstone.

Yellowstone's birds include owls and trumpeter swans.

tiny wrens and giant trumpeter swans whose wings stretch 8 ft. (2.4 m) across.

Yellowstone's lakes and streams are cold and clean and alive with fish, including the rare Montana grayling. The Yellowstone cutthroat trout is found nowhere else on Earth.

Lakes and Landscapes

Yellowstone Lake is 20 miles (32 kilometers) long and very deep. It was formed by ancient rivers of ice, called glaciers, sliding down from the surrounding mountains.

The Yellowstone River flows through Yellowstone Lake. Over thousands of years, its rushing

Yellowstone Lake (top); the Yellowstone River (middle), which runs through the Grand Canyon of the Yellowstone; and Lower Yellowstone Falls (bottom)

water carved an awesome gash, 1,500 ft. (457 m) deep, through solid rock. This is the Grand Canyon of the Yellowstone.

Down in that canyon are the park's two largest waterfalls. While Upper Yellowstone Falls is "only" as high as an 11-story building, Lower Yellowstone Falls is as tall as a 31-story skyscraper!

Yellowstone National Park is gigantic, protecting 3,384 square miles (8,765 square kilometers) of scenic mountains and valleys. Most of this is wilderness land,

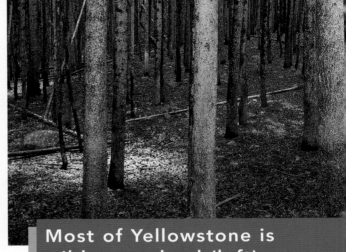

Most of Yellowstone is wilderness land (left). Yellowstone has many forests of lodgepole pine (right).

where no roads, buildings, or machines are allowed.

Much of Yellowstone is covered with forests of lodgepole pine. Because their trunks are straight and strong, Indians used these slender pines to make the poles for their *tipis*, or lodges.

Fire

Natural fires—those caused by lightning rather than by humans— actually help keep forests healthy. They destroy old, dead timber and fertilize the soil with ash. That's why Yellowstone's policy is to let natural fires burn unless they endanger human life or property.

After the fires of 1988, new lush growth sprang up at Yellowstone.

In 1988, wildfires roared across Yellowstone Park, thinning the forests and creating sunny new meadows, rich with grasses, wildflowers, and brush. This new vegetation provides food for bison, elk, deer, and pronghorn—which, in turn, feed wolves, bears, coyotes, and other animals.

Indians, Explorers— and You!

Yellowstone has a long and exciting human history. For thousands of years, American Indians visited this magical place. Here they hunted, fished, and collected obsidian—a hard, black, volcanic rock that they used to make arrowheads.

American Indians made tools from the obsidian they found in the Yellowstone region (left). Few people believed early explorers' stories about the strange wonders of Yellowstone (right).

In the early 1800s, white explorers discovered Yellowstone. When John Colter, Jim Bridger, Osborne Russell, and others returned home and told of the strange and wonderful things they had seen, nobody believed them!

But settlers soon began flooding into Yellowstone to hunt, log, ranch, and mine. Suddenly, this precious American jewel was in danger of being stolen by a few greedy people.

On March 1, 1872, President Ulysses S. Grant signed a bill making Yellowstone the world's first national park. This assured that the beauty, wildlife, and thermal wonders of this special place would be protected forever.

Today, there's so much to see and do at Yellowstone, it's hard to know where to start. You don't want to miss the steaming, gushing, bubbling thermal features. And Yellowstone is one of the best places in the United States for watching and photographing wild animals. You can also hike, camp, fish, take a horseback or stagecoach ride, tour the visitors' centers, or become a Junior Ranger.

Yellowstone winters are cold, with so much snow that most of the park's roads are closed. The summer crowds are gone and the bears are snoring in their dens. But bison, elk, wolves, and many other animals remain active. Now is the time to explore the silent white park on cross-country skis.

A herd of elk at Mammoth Hot Springs (left) and bison in winter at Yellowstone (below)

However and whenever you visit Yellowstone National Park, you'll have fun, learn a lot, and see things you never dreamed possible.

To Find Out More

Here are some additional resources to help you learn more about Yellowstone National Park:

 **Books**

Knapp, Patty. **Getting to Know Yellowstone National Park.** M. I. Adventure Publications, 1997.

Lauber, Patricia. **Summer of Fire: Yellowstone 1988.** Orchard Books, 1991.

Tesar, Jenny E. **America's Top 10 National Parks.** Blackbirch Marketing, 1998.

Weber, Michael. **Our National Parks.** Millbrook Press, 1995.

Organizations and Online Sites

Greater Yellowstone Coalition
http://www.greater yellowstone.org/

Find out how you can help protect the world's first national park.

National Parks Conservation Association
1300 Nineteenth St. NW
Washington, D.C. 20036

An organization founded to help protect the nation's parks for future generations.

National Park Service: ParkNet
http://www.nps.gov/

Official information on the National Park Service, with links to all national park websites.

The Yellowstone Association
P.O. Box 117
Yellowstone National Park, WY 82190
307/344-7381
Yellowstoneassociation.org/

Here you can order books, maps, videos and other park publications, as well as information on the Yellowstone Institute, which offers year-round education programs.

Important Words

algae very tiny plants that live in water

ancient very old

aquatic living in or having to do with water

bacteria tiny, one-celled organisms

bull adult male of certain large animals

erosion slow wearing away of rock or other material by water, wind, ice, and other natural forces

minerals materials that make up rocks

native belonging to a certain place

petrified turned to stone

spew to pour forth

wilderness unspoiled place filled with wild and natural landscapes, plants, and animals

Index

Meet the Author

David Petersen lives in a cabin in the Colorado mountains. He has been exploring Yellowstone National Park since he was old enough to crawl. David also writes adult books about nature, including *The Nearby Faraway: A Personal Journey Through the Heart of the West* (Johnson Books).